AF521073

Beginners' Programme
to
Plectrum Guitar
(Grade-0)

Beginners' Programme
to
Plectrum Guitar
(Grade-0)

By

Kapil Srivastava

(Guitarmonk)

UNICORN BOOKS

Publishers
UNICORN BOOKS
F-2/16, Ansari Road, Daryaganj, New Delhi-110002
☎ 23275434, 23262683, 23262783 • Fax: 011-23257790
E-mail: info@unicornbooks.in • *Website:* www.unicornbooks.in

ISBN 978-81-7806-221-1

Edition: 2018

Printed at : Param Offsetters, Okhla, New Delhi-110020

Preface

I have great pleasure to bring forth this book as part of my endeavour to give some sort of organisation and structure to the music education in India.

Going by my professional experience in the last two decades, I have realized that India badly needs an organized music teaching system. The non-existence of such a system is one of the factors that plagues music education in our country. Non-compulsory music education and lack of awareness are the other factors which add to its present state.

This is the first book of the four volume book series published under the same title. As there is a dearth of constructive content for study and reference on this subject, to a great extent, this book will serve the purpose. The well organized content and the exercises of this book are a first-class study material for the aspiring students of music to prepare for various examinations. Even a 5 year old learner can use this book and it will help him to achieve the desired goal in a short span of time.

It is a matter of great pride and pleasure to note that my other books on music are well received by students and readers alike across the globe. They are also introduced as text books in many schools. We reach out all the places and regions through these books and thus we would be able to serve you without our physical presence.

I thank readers, students and others for their support and patronage. Your suggestions and comments on the further improvement of this book will be thankfully acknowledged and the same will be incorporated in the next edition.

Author

Overview

THE OBJECTIVES

The primary objective of this book is to familiarise the learners with terminologies, exercises and repertoires along with the audios of the compositions. This would help the learners to get a clear perspective on various aspects of the subject.

WHOM IS THIS BOOK FOR?

The book is for complete beginners who know nothing about the instrument, the students who prepare for examinations and the teachers who train the students.

THE SPECIAL FEATURES

- It is customized into levels and can be covered very easily in 12-24 sessions maximum based on time involvement.
- It is an ideal book for teachers who help their student in constructive sessions and productive outcome.
- The book is a step-by-step guide which takes a student from one level to the next. It also inspires success at every grade via achievements which motivates students to get curious and interested in further learning.
- This book contains an audio-CD that instructs on speed and movement of tune: and it is a good reference for the learners who find difficulties in staff reading.
- It contains the basics of staff notations which is very useful information for any music beginner.
- It is a compilation of very significant compositions, rated at a global standard, essential for any music student.

- It offers finger movements which are the most important part for a quality and right learning and support to both teacher and student.
- It offers exercise, pop music repertoire, music theory and Practice Compositions

HOW WILL THIS BOOK HELP YOU?

- It can help you in going about a step-by-step and systematic learning
- A quality and constructive repertoire of songs for your personal performance.
- It instructs you on finger patterns, so as to help both teacher and student with accurate fingering.
- You can expect a basic performance from yourself and can render a medley of tunes on any platform after practicing the given tunes.
- It can assist you, to a great extent, for a performance preparation and content and, thus, it can bring out a musician in you.

Content

WHAT IS A GUITAR?

A guitar is a stringed music instrument which is played with both fingers and plectrum, (Pick, Striker) and the music is produced by vibration of strings. There are evidences to suggest that the use of guitar dates back to 15th centaury in Spain. It has passed through many stages of its development and progress over many years. This instrument appeals the music lovers and others alike. In olden days, guitar was mostly used as an accompaniment instrument, whereas, today it is also used as a solo instrument extensively. Guitar is a major part of recordings, orchestras and pop concerts and as it is independent enough to render several music genres of the world.

WHAT MAKES GUITAR UNIQUE

It is one of the most musical and versatile instruments because a guitar can be used for playing various music styles such as Classical, Pop, Jazz, Rock, Blues, Country, Folk and now Ragas (Indian Classical). Unlike other lead instruments such as violin, sitar, flute, saxophone etc, which are used for playing lead tunes or with the accompaniment/percussion instruments as drums, tabla etc., a guitar can be used either way, i.e. if you want to sing along with it or may want to use guitar alone. It is a major part of recordings, orchestras and pop concerts and as it is independent enough to render several music genres of the world. These features make guitar one of the most valuable and contemporary instruments in demand and priority. In short, no other musical instrument is as multifarious as a guitar.

WHEN CAN YOU LEARN GUITAR?

Though age is no bar for learning music yet it is advised that a learner of guitar should be around 10 years because it demands some degree of finger-muscle-strength. Moreover, to practice it efficiently, you need to work upon technical aspects of guitar both in theory and practice.

TYPES OF GUITAR

Guitar comes in various types, shapes, brands, models, sizes, colors, category as Classical, Electric, Acoustic, Acoustic-Electric, Jumbo Folk, Standard Folk, Slim Body, F-Cut shape, Arch-top.

Guitars can also be categorized on the basis of number of strings such as 12 strings, 6 strings (the standard one), 7 strings, 5 strings, 4 strings (Tenor, Bass Guitar), 10 strings and now modern guitarists are going with customized strings to get what they want to produce in their guitar.

Guitar has one more categorization as per the strings quality i.e. Steel String, Nylon String etc.

- STEEL STRING GUITAR (ACOUSTIC)
- ELECTRIC GUITAR
- NYLON STRING GUITAR (ACOUSTIC)
- BASS GUITAR (ELECTRIC)
- TENOR GUITAR

CLASSICAL GUITAR

The classical guitar has nylon strings and it's a 6-string guitar. It is also known as Nylon String guitar. Classical guitar has a round hole and a wider neck to allow the right hand fingers to easily adapt fingers-style playing. This guitar has a lighter string tension and greater string gauge; the wider distance of each string makes easier movement for fingers in comparison to steel-string guitar. The wood on classical guitar is usually lighter than folk guitars to help the tone production from Nylon strings.

ELECTRIC GUITAR

This guitar is also known as Solid Body Electric Guitar. It produces sound through the amplifiers and doesn't have a Sound Box. The guitar has a smoother sound fret-board and string gauges may vary depending upon the style of music. It's mostly seen in Rock Music. The Electric guitar has greater possibilities of sound variations, tones depending upon the gadgets used with the amplification.

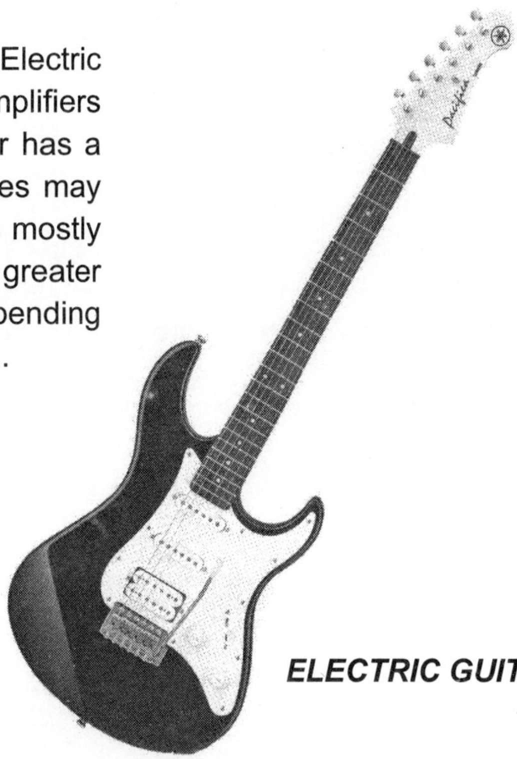

ELECTRIC GUITAR

STANDARD GUITAR

STANDARD SPANISH GUITAR

This is the most commonly used acoustic guitar. A narrow fretboard and steel strings make it different from the classical guitar. The standard Spanish guitars comes in attractive bodies, sizes, shapes and colors i.e. from slim, medium to jumbo. It is also known as steel-string guitar.

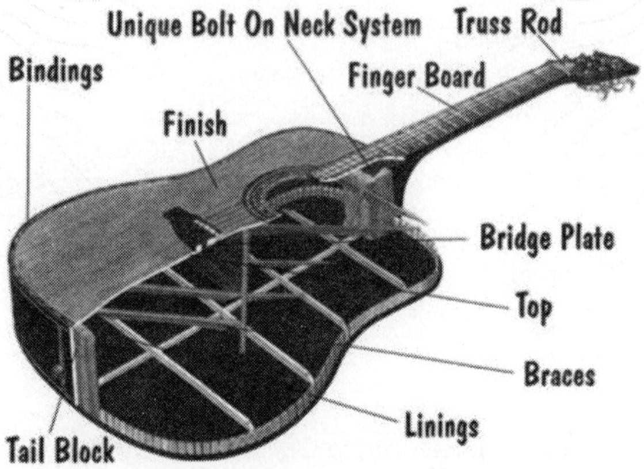

ANATOMY OF GUITAR

Image Courtesy: www.phys.unsw.edu.au

ACOUSTIC GUITAR

1. Headstock
2. Tuning Machines
3. Nut
4. Fret
5. Sound hole
6. Bridge Saddle
7. Fretboard
8. Strings

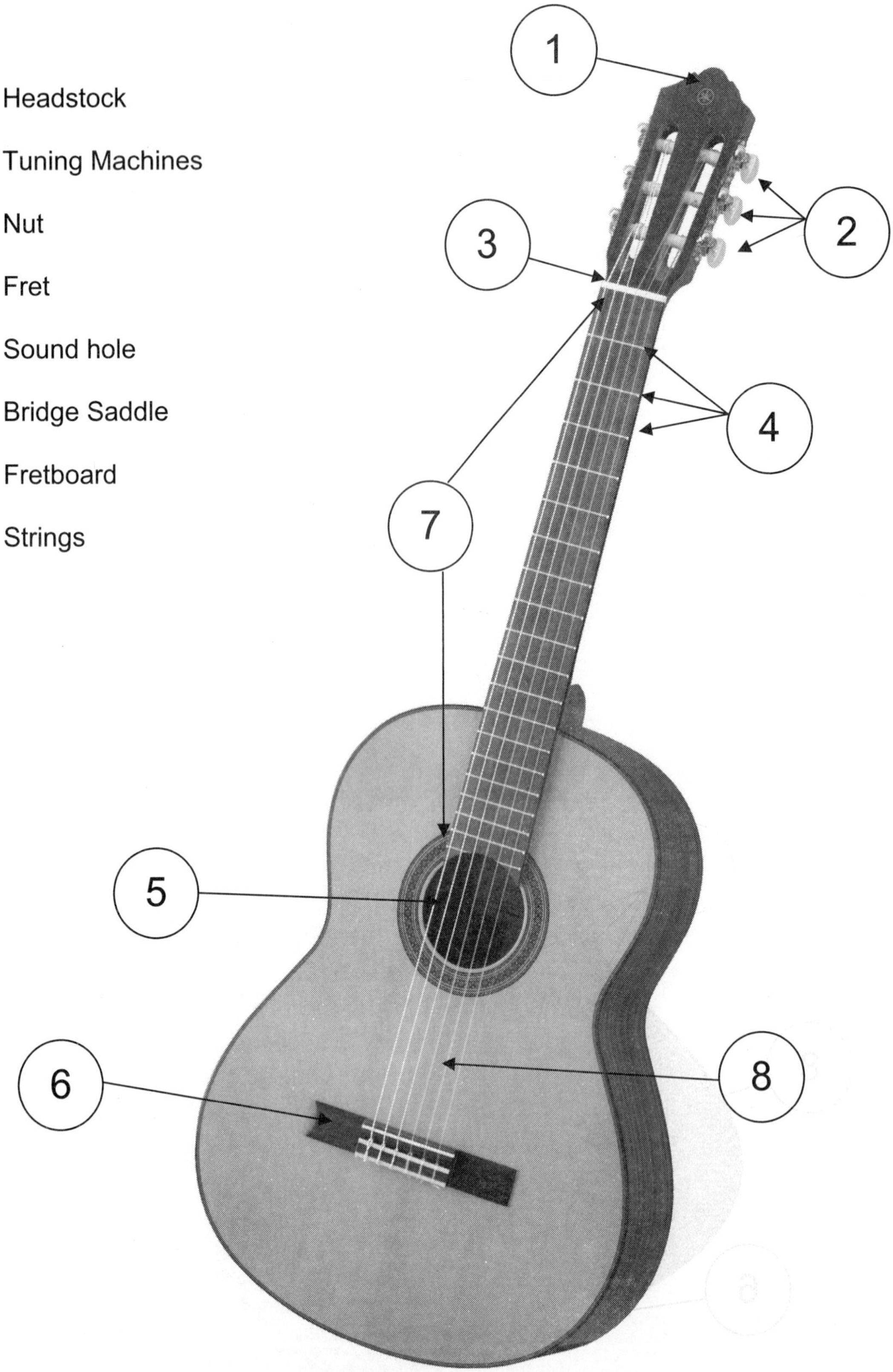

Suggested Reading, Reference Guide: ***Step by Step Beginner's Guide to Spanish Guitar***
(Author: Kapil Srivastava) – www.kapilsrivastava.com

ELECTRIC GUITAR

1. Headstock
2. Tuning Machines
3. Nut
4. Fret
5. Belt Pin
6. End Pin
7. Volume Knob
8. Bridge
9. Strings
10. Pick up

PLECTRUM

The plectrum also known as striker or pick is used to hit the guitar strings. The hitting of strings is described as plucking, picking or stroking.

Plectrum comes in wide variety of shapes, sizes, materials, colours and quality. As per thickness they can be categorized into 3 types as thin or light, medium and hard.

HOLDING SPECTRUM

The plectrum is held between two fingers of the right as shown in the figure. The two most important strokes by a plectrum is known as UPSTROKE and DOWNSTROKE.

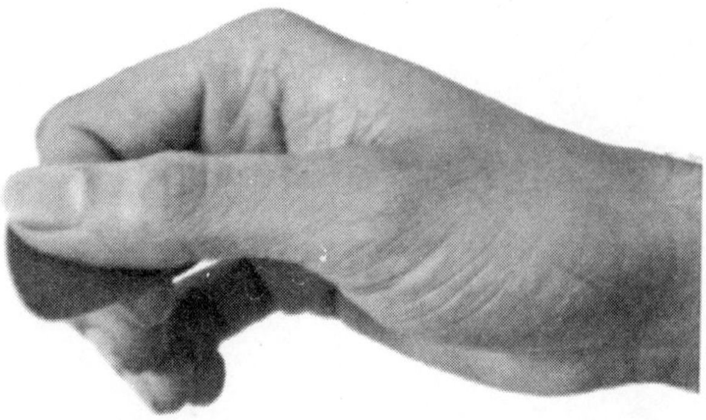

Plectrums are manufactured in a plethora of brands.

SITTING POSTURE

There are 2 basic postures to hold a guitar- the classical way and other is the casual way. For standard guitar learning, the students have freedom for casual ways as shown in the figures below:

Casual Way - 1

Casual Way - 2

Suggested Reading, Reference Guide: ***Step by Step Beginner's Guide to Spanish Guitar*** (Author: Kapil Srivastava) – www.kapilsrivastava.com

KNOW YOUR FRETBOARD

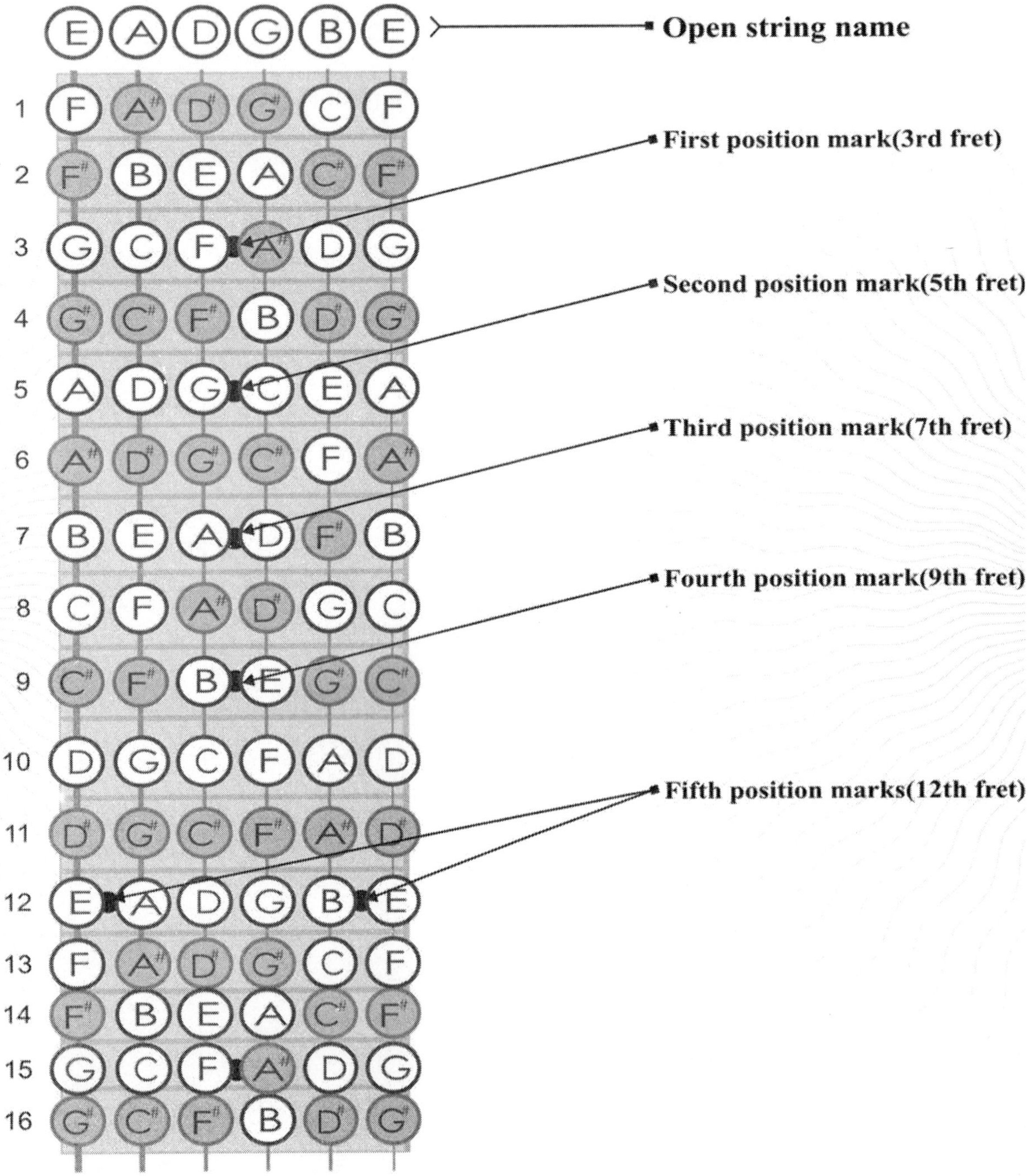

Suggested Reading, Reference Guide: ***Step by Step Beginner's Guide to Spanish Guitar***
(Author: Kapil Srivastava) – www.kapilsrivastava.com

DEFINITIONS AND TERMINOLOGIES

- **Note:** A note is a name given to describe a particular music frequency or pitch. There are 12 notes in music described with the help of 7 names as:-

  A B C D E F G

  The remaining 5 notes are defined by using Sharp or Flat symbols.

  So there are total 12 notes in music as:

  A, A#/Bb, B, C, C#/Db, D, D#/Eb, E, F, F#/Gb, G, G#/Ab

- **Interval:** An interval refers to distance (musical distance) between any two notes. The two most important intervals are *half tone* (least music interval) and *whole tone* (equals 2 half tones).

- **Scale:** The word Scale derived from the Latin word 'Scale' meaning ladder. So just like a ladder, Scale is a series of steps of notes that can be taken in ascending and descending order.

- **Sharp:** A Sharp symbol ***(#)*** raises the frequency of a note by halftone/semitone. The suffice sharp is used for a black key to the right of (or higher than) white key.

- **Flat:** A Flat symbol ***(b)*** decreases the frequency of a note by halftone/semitone. The suffice flat is used for a black key to the left of (or lower than) a white key.

- **Tempo:** It defines the speed of beat per minute.

- **Chords:** A combination of three or more notes played simultaneously. In layman terms, chords are the part of music being played at the background i.e. over the melody line, as the background music.
  - Chords can be classified into two main categories: -
    - 1) Major chords also known as *Primary Chords*
    - 2) Minor chords also known as *Secondary Chords*

- **Octave**: It is the eighth tone above a given pitch having twice as many vibrations per second. It can also be the eighth tone below a given pitch with half as many vibrations per second.

- **Staff:** Staff consists of five horizontal lines parallel to each other having four spaces. Plenty of symbols are placed over it to express the music. Appropriate music symbols, depending upon the intended effect, are placed on the staff according to their corresponding pitch or function.

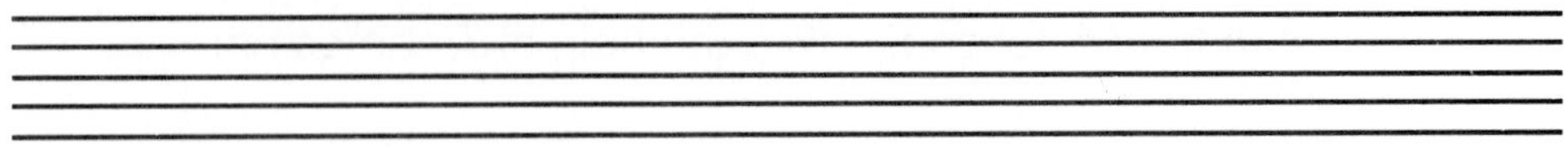

- **Lines and Spaces:** The lines and spaces are numbered from bottom to top; the bottom line is the first line and the top line is the fifth line.

- **Clef:** A symbol placed at the beginning of the staff that indicates and fixes the pitch of the notes over the staff.

- **Treble Clef (or G clef):** Generally, the treble clef signals notes to be played by the right hand and this clef is also called the G clef as shown.

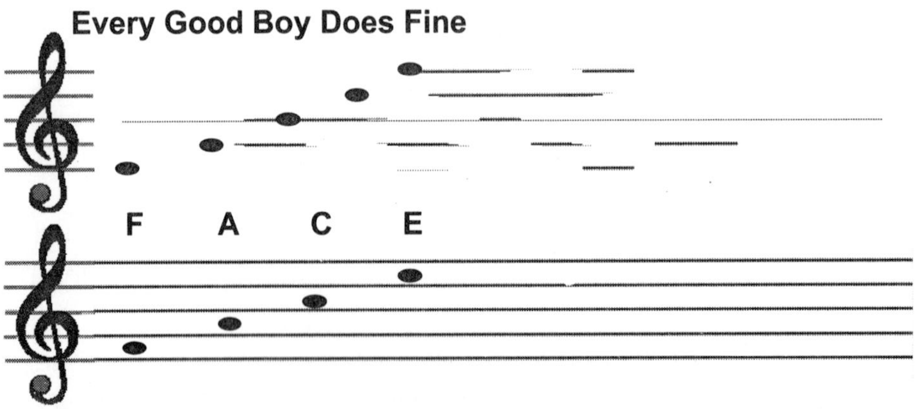

- **Bass Clef (or F clef):** Your left hand plays the lower notes on the keyboard, which are also called bass notes and the clef representing them is called as Bass Clef or F clef.

- **Note Value:** A note value indicates the relative duration of a note, using the colour or shape of the note head, the presence or absence of a stem, and the presence or absence of flags/beams.

- When a **stem** is present, it can go either up (from the right side of the note head) or down (from the left side). In most cases, the stem goes down if the note-head is on the center line or above, and up otherwise. Any flags/tail always goes to the right of the stem.

- **Beams:** When two or more notes which would normally have flags (eighth notes or shorter) appear successively, the flags may be replaced by beams as shown:

Name	*Note*	Rests
Whole Note *or* Semibreve	𝅝	𝄻
Half Note *or* Minim	𝅗𝅥	𝄼
Quarter Note *or* Crochet	♩	𝄽
Eighth Note *or* Quaver	♪	𝄾
Sixteenth Note *or* Semiquaver	𝅘𝅥𝅯	𝄿

- **Measures/Bars:** Grouping of the beats into small batches till the bar ends. Each measure has a specific number of beats depending upon the composer's feel behind the melody.

- **Barline:** Differentiating each measure (containing beats) with a vertical line is called *Barline* as shown:
- **Single Barline:** Go on to the single measure.
- **Double Barline:** Go on to the next section of the song, which will have a change, whether it's a new tempo, new grouping of beats per measure?
- **Repeat (one thin and one thick Barline, plus two dots):** Repeat the music from the beginning of the song.
- **End (one thin and one thick Barline):** Reached at the end of the song.
- **Time Signature:** Expresses the number of beats and nature of note to be used in a bar. It is expressed in fraction form wherein the top number shows how many beats there will be in a bar and the bottom number shows what kind of beats they will be.
- **Key Signature:** The sharps or flats symbols placed at the beginning of the staff.
- **Ledger lines:** Short lines placed above and below the staff to reach the pitches of the composition that are beyond the range of staff.
- **Staccato:** It is indicated by a dot over or under a note, means shortening of a note.
- **Da Capo (D.C.)**: To repeat from a composition from the beginning.
- **Da Capo al fine (D.C. al fine)**: To repeat from the beginning up to the word ***fine***.
- **Dal Segno (D.S.):** To repeat from the sign ***$.***

GUITAR STYLES: PLECTRUM VS FINGER PICKING STYLE

This particular topic is as hot as it was before. The guitar genre has developed so widely during last few decades that guitar teachers are being compared now by their choice of genres, which is totally wrong on the part of audience or student.

The growing perception in masses influencing a student's/amateur's interest to choose a particular style as hip-hop, rock, blues, classical etc. on the basis of popularity rather via right understanding. The student generally adapts a particular style or learning because of its mass popularity but they must not undermine the standard education as it can make them adapt to any style in guitar.

Basically there are two main styles of playing as Finger Picking (classical) and Plectrum Playing. Fingering picking is an independent genre and it's recommended that a student should not learn this guitar if he has a taste for classical music otherwise chances are high that at a later stage the student will drop this style because he feels too bored by hardcore practice required to build this style. Mostly students get attracted to the look and feel of this guitarring but they don't see the time commitment and sacrifice required for it. The inspiration should come from a personal taste rather impressiveness of style because that personal taste will keep a student learning.

Plectrum playing is more commercial as it goes to pop, rock, blues, and folk music. It's not only entertaining but commercially popular also. Both genres have some technical advantage and each style has its own popularity, qualities and features. Each style demands time devotion and practice. Classical guitar is more of a solo playing that demands years of efforts to reach at a good level whereas plectrum guitar can reward you with much output in shorter time.

At a later stage and if one is committed, some guitarists can adapt to both styles based on their time factor. At last, it's a question of goal and personal interest.

Some of the well known guitar genres are: Classical, Plectrum, Rock, Blues, Jazz, Country, Pop, Folk, and Ragas etc. Some of the wellknown guitar players are Jimi Hendrix, Duane Allman, Eric Clapton, B.B.King, Chuck Berry, Stevie Ray Vaughan, Carlos Santana, George Harrison, John McLaughlin etc.

GUITAR MAINTENANCE TIPS

- Don't expose yours guitar to direct heat or to dewdrops in the night. Don't place it before a heater, a heat ventilator, a radiator or an air-conditioner.
- Never tune the strings higher to the standard pitch. You must have the pitch note with you to tune the guitar.
- While tuning guitar, tight the strings by slowly rotating the tuning pegs and not rapidly as it may break the string.
- Protect yours guitar from dust and always cover it when not playing.
- Keep a soft cotton cloth to wipe the sweat of fingers over the frets and strings. Do it during and after playing the guitar.

- Change the strings at least once in two months, though not necessary. In most cases they may require change or you may change them when the strings are rusted.

- Loosen all the strings tension from the standard pitch, especially when not playing the guitar for a period, which may be a week or more.

- It's always better to change the worn out strings as once a string is worn out it sounds dead. Some guitarist use sandpaper for polishing to remove the rust but it destroys the tone quality.

- For better maintenance and efficiency, one must keep an extra string set, a tool that can cut the strings, pick holder, music stand, and plectrums in varied thickness, cotton cloth and guitar cover or case.

Also take special care from the bumps and kicks while carrying the guitar on a bike or in a car. It has been observed and experienced that most of the guitars are damaged in the course of their journey on two-wheelers. Belt buckles can also destroy the back finish of a guitar. One can use double or triple covers while carrying it on a bike. It assures extra safety.

WHY MUSIC

Music learning enhances several qualities in the learners such as problem solving, teamwork, goal setting, self-expression, coordination, memory skills, self-confidence, esteem, concentration and poise. Music learning also improves organizational skills as how to organize tasks and time-management etc.

The benefits of learning music can be seen in one's personal as well as professional life. These benefits can be classified into four categories as given below.

Physiological as coordination between mind and muscles, hands-eye coordination, development of fine motor skills

Mental Benefits

Encourages creativity, concentration and focus, use of left and right brain, intellectual stimulation, self-control

Emotional Benefits

Aesthetic appreciation, emotional expression, self-confidence, feeling of accomplishment, spiritual experience

Social Benefits
Shared activity and communication, performing for an audience, music is an international language, a sense of pride and accomplishment

Effects of Music on Brain
Several studies have been conducted about effects of music on one's brain. Scientists have observed that children who are exposed to music or who plays a musical instrument perform better in academics than other students who don't participate in musical activity. Music learning helps in IQ, vocabulary and development of certain parts of brain.

The very best engineers and technical designers in the Silicon Valley industry are, nearly without exception, practising musicians. Music training can enhance brain functions.

A research team exploring the link between music and intelligence reported that music training is far superior to computer instruction in dramatically enhancing children's abstract reasoning skills, the skills necessary for learning math and science.

The musician is constantly adjusting decisions on tempo, tone, style, rhythm, phrasing, and feeling, training the brain to become incredibly good at organizing and conducting numerous activities at once.

THE POWER OF MUSIC

The man that hath no music in himself, Nor is not moved with concord of sweet sounds, is fit for treasons, stratagems and spoils.

–William Shakespeare

MUSIC THERAPY

Scientific studies have attempted to measure the potential benefits of music and have found:

- Music has a beneficial effect on our physiological functions, slowing the pulse and heart rate, lowering blood pressure, and decreasing the levels of stress hormones.
- Music's form and structure can bring order, encouraging coordination and communication
- Not only reduces stress, anxiety but also helps relieve depression and increase self-esteem.
- Reduce burnout and improves mood
- Significantly reduces emotional distress and boosts quality of life
- Music is a significant mood-changer and reliever of stress.

“The soothing power of music is well-established, and has been used for hundreds of years to treat illnesses and restore harmony between mind and body. It has a unique link to our emotions, thus being an extremely effective stress management tool.”

"Play a tune on the guitar and sing along. That works even in the worst of times. By the time I'm done with the song, I've breathed deep, I've controlled myself to some degree to be able to sing on key :-), and I've come back into myself, and more into the real time moment." – Anonymous

Facts about Corporate Stress

- Average 12.8 million working days are lost to stress, depression and anxiety and approximately 5 million people in the UK feel “very” or “extremely” stressed by their work. One can conclude that how big this loss is to the ideal productivity.
- The Confederation of British Industry estimates businesses lost £10.2 billion average per year through lost productivity caused by stress.
- Research from Harvard University observes that work stress is as harmful to health as smoking or taking no exercise.
- According to the American Academy of Family Physicians, two-thirds of office visits to family doctors are for stress-related symptoms.
- Almost everyone experiences events that they find difficult to cope with. In a recent poll, 89 per cent of people said they had experienced serious stress in their lives.
- Stress-related mental disorders have been called the fastest-growing occupational (work-related) disease in the U.S.
- Your health is in your hands. Far-sighted employers now provide their employees with tools to manage stress - from paying for therapists to visit their premises offering onsite massage and other powerful holistic treatments to arranging seminars to educate their employees to manage stress effectively.

(Source: Worldwide web)

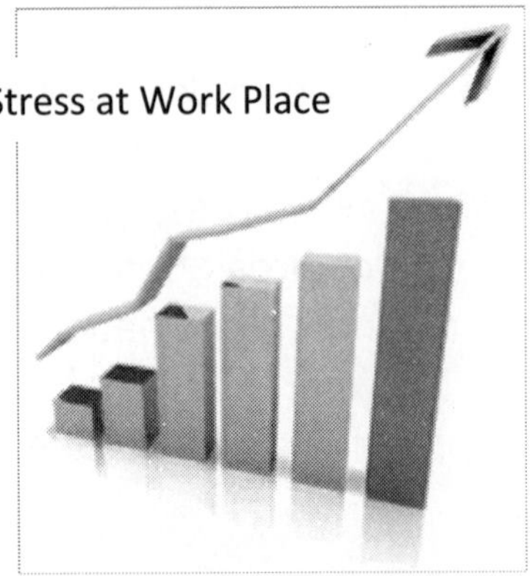

Benefits of Corporate Music Workshop

- Improved Employee Engagement
- Reduced Absenteeism
- Enhanced Customer Service
- Improved Performance
- Reduced Attrition
- Enhanced Quality of Work
- Improved Team Interaction
- Reduced Grievances
- Reduced Tardiness

Some Music Cure

The classical compositions (ragas) of music create deep impact on our mind and emotions.

Diseases	*Relative Ragas*
• Insomnia (sleeplessness)	Puriya
• Asthma, chronic cold, cough, tuberculosis, Sinus and chest related problems	Bhairavi
• Anger, mental instability	Malhar
• Impurities of blood an	Asavari
• d relative diseases	
• Mental disorders and impatience	Saurat & Jaijaivanti
• Mental concentration, liver ailments	Hindola

Anti-Stress Music Album: Guitarmonk has produced series of Raga-Based Albums name as **'Kayotsarg'** and they are used as an anti-stress tool at many corporate companies. For information about licenses, albums please email at guitarmonk.info@gmail.com

MUSIC IN SCHOOLS

The existing music education system of schools in India has several limitations:

- Music objectives, curricula, benefits are not clearly defined; music is just for the sake of formality without anyone owning responsibility to it.
- Musical intelligence/understanding is terribly missing in majority of schools which is directly and indirectly affecting the students' personality growth.
- Lack of standardized curriculums and organized/trained teachers who are able to cater international and general parameters.
- Music is not considered as a core academic subject but a part-time activity
- Lack of standardized university level system to train teachers to impart quality music education.
- School kids learn music outside the school premises
- School music education is only limited to 2 to10 percent kids who are good at music. In some schools sports are so dominant that music is taken disrespectfully and by granted.
- Most prodigies miss their school support in catering their interest and talent.
- Absence of basic philosophy and guide which should direct the music programme..

Objectives of Music Education

- To imbibe in them a complete personality growth at a realistic level.
- To relate music learning with visible & practical benefits in students' personality at every level of education and contribute its benefits in overall sphere of their life as academic education, society, family, emotional well being, aesthetical appreciation, friendly and loving environment.
- To cover the core competency skills and standardized concepts at different levels of education
- To let them perform individually and as a group (ensembles)
- To demonstrate music learning through positive attitudes, skills and lifelong learning to occur in every sphere of academics, social and spiritual growth.

COMPOSITIONS

(A collection of special practice repertoire...)

Brother John Sing and Play

Plectrum Guitar, Guitarmonk

Melody
Chords
G
G
G
G
Melody
Chords
G
G
G
G

Ode to Joy

Plectrum Guitar

Symphony Theme by L.V. Beethoven

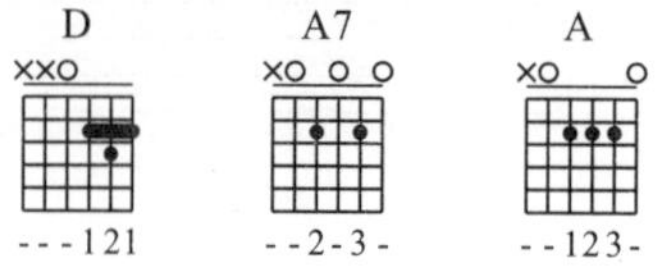

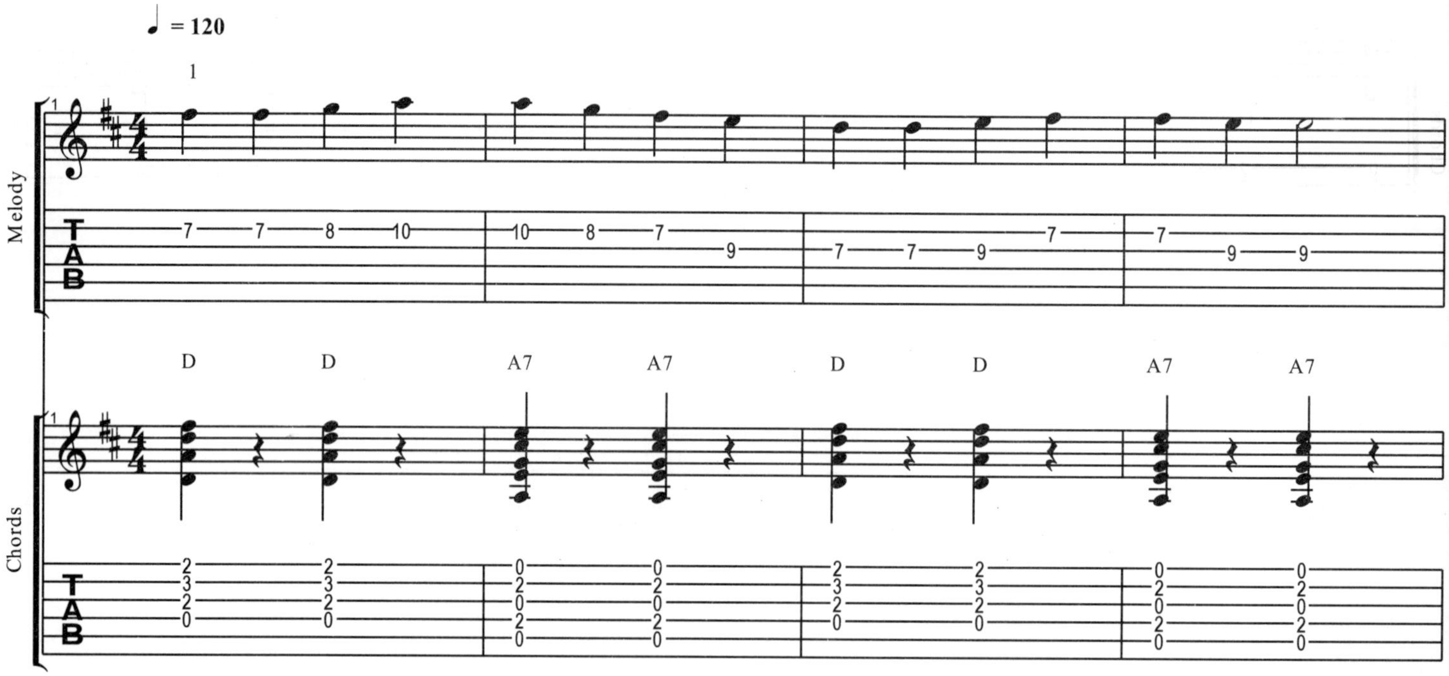

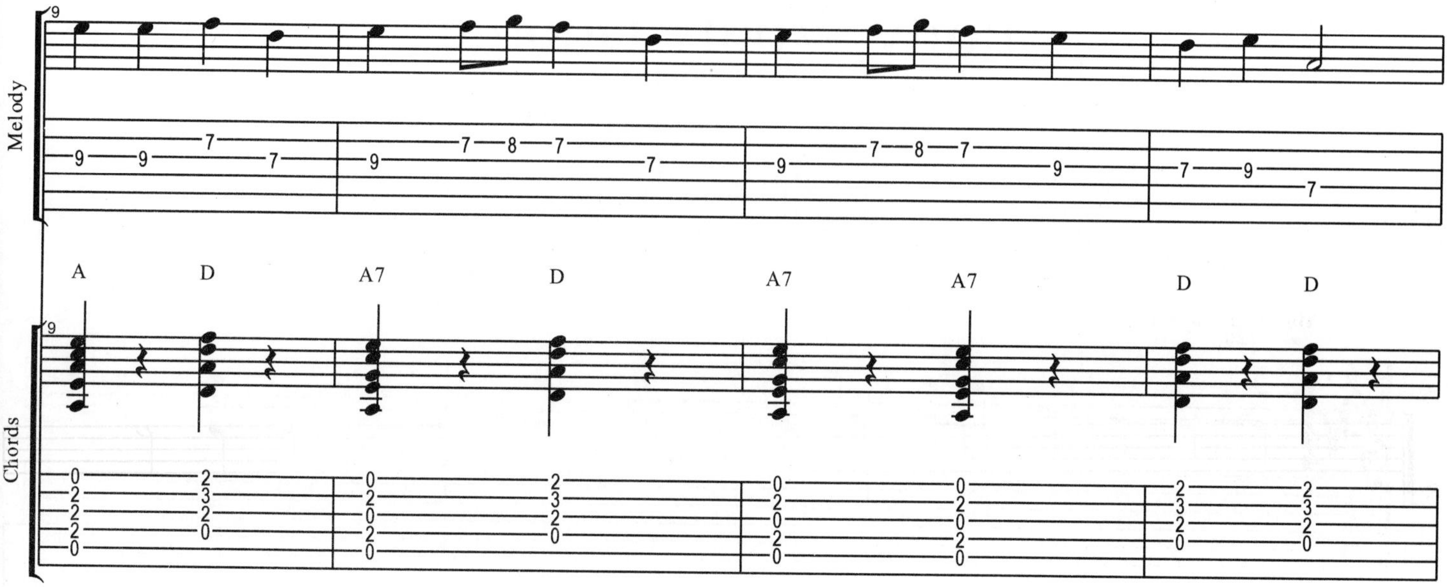
9
Melody
A D A7 D A7 A7 D D
9
Chords

Melody
D D A7 A7 D D A7 D
Chords

Polly Wooly Doodle

Plectrum Guitar, Guitarmonk

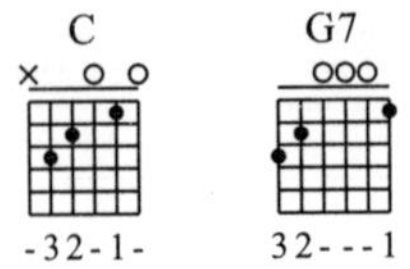

Moderate ♩ = 100

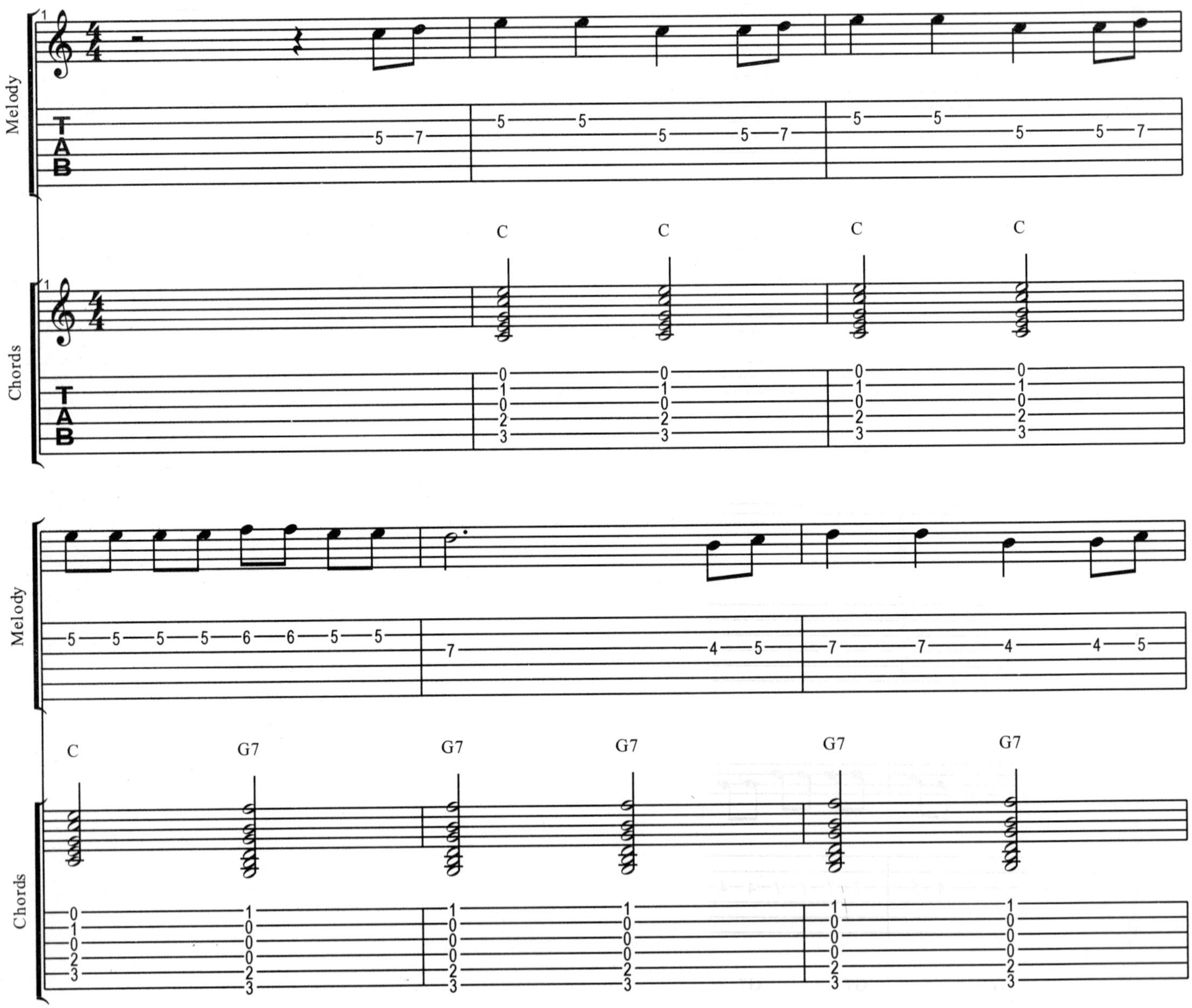

Melody
Chords
G7 G7 G7 G7 C C
C C C C C G7
G7 G7 G7 G7 G7 G7 G7 G7 C

Ten Little Indians

Plectrum Guitar, Guitarmonk

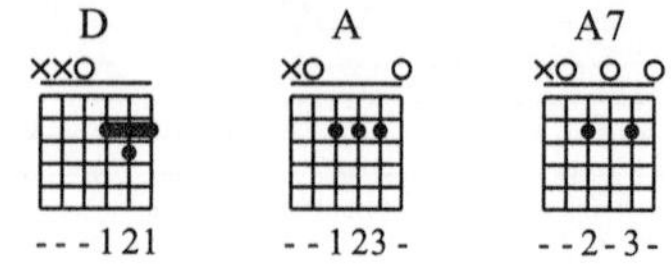

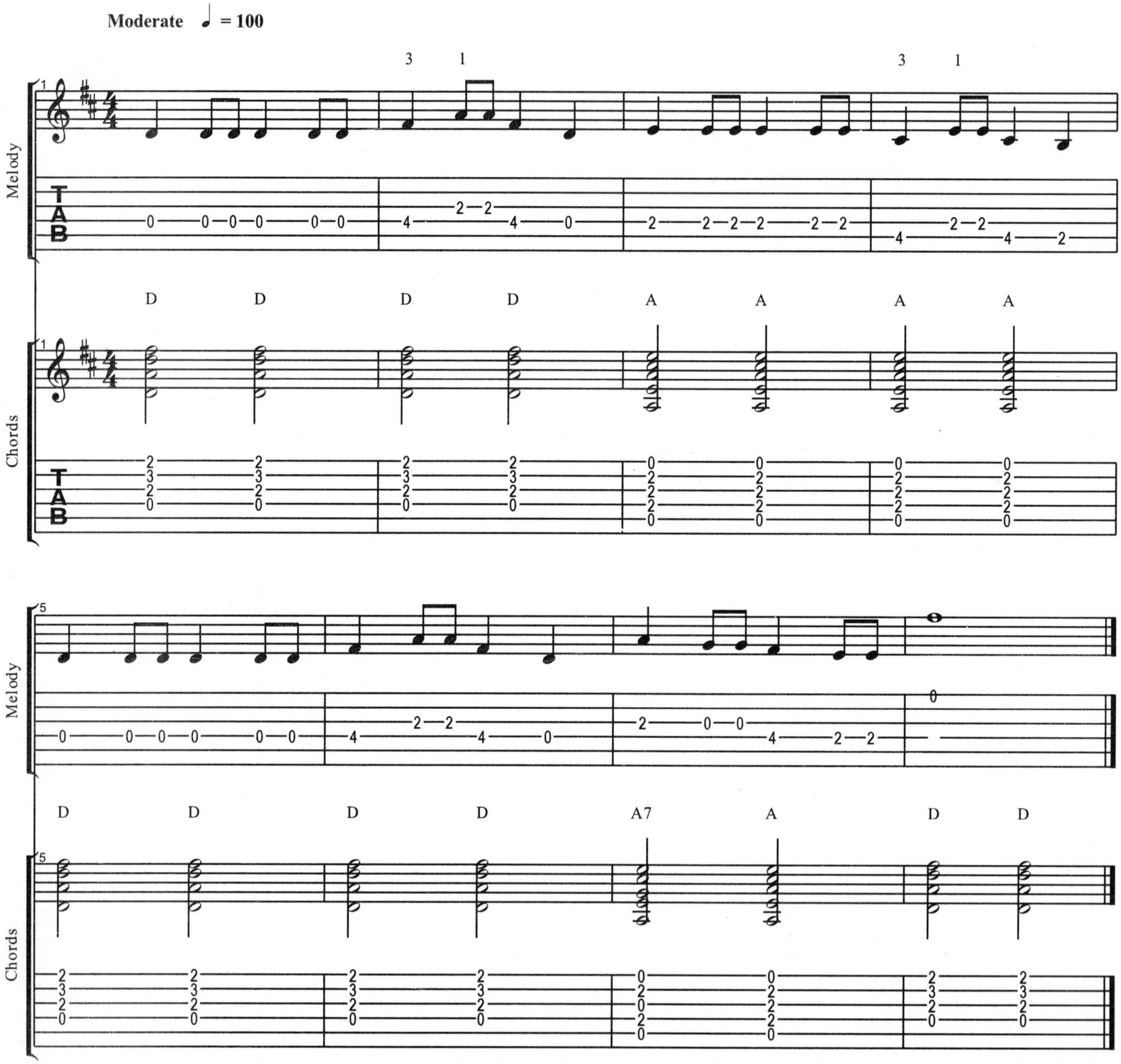

Twinkle Twinkle

Plectrum Guitar, Guitarmonk

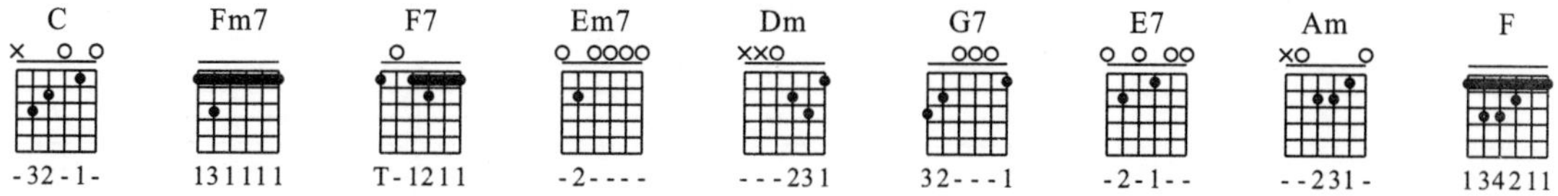

Melody
Chords
C
C G7 C D7 G G7 C C C C
Fm7 F7 Em7 Dm G7 E7 Am F G7 C
F7M F7 Em7 A7 Dm G7 E7 Am F G7 C

Airtel Theme

Plectrum Guitar, Guitarmonk

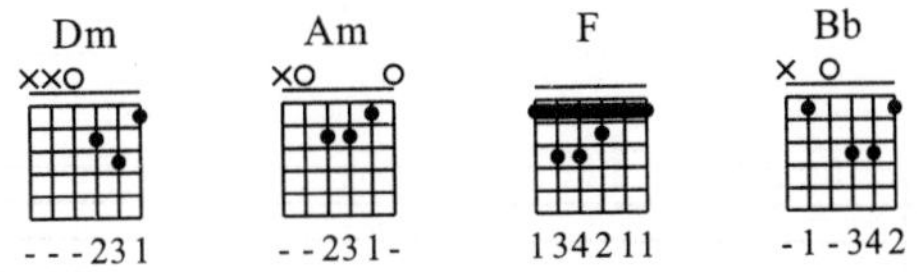

Melody
Chords
Dm Dm Dm Dm F F
Melody
Chords
Am Am Bb Bb Dm Dm

Zacchaeus

Plectrum Guitar, Guitarmonk

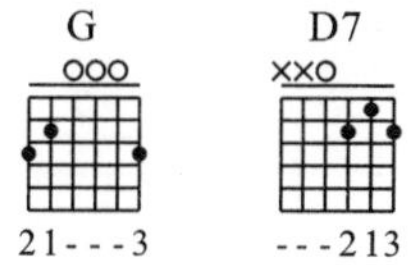

Moderate ♩ = 92

Melody
Chords
G D7 G D7 G D7 G
Melody
Chords
G D7 G G D7 G

Happy Birthday

Plectrum Guitar, Guitarmonk

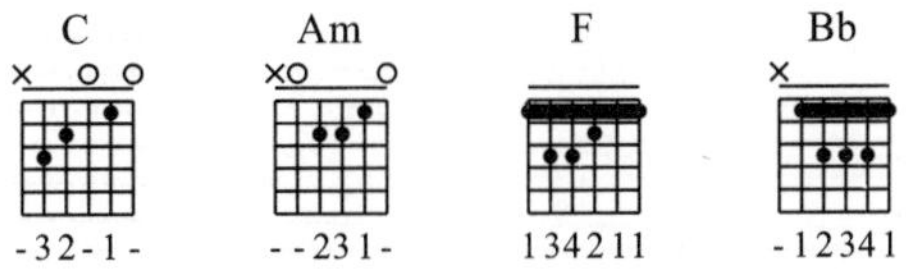

Moderate ♩ = 116

F C C
Melody
F C Am C
Chords
F Bb F
Melody
F F Bb Bb F
Chords

Hush little baby

Plectrum Guitar, Guitarmonk

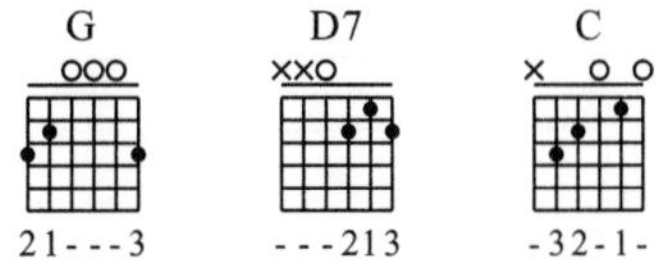

Moderate ♩ = 80

Melody
Chords
G G D7 D7 D7 D7 C G
Melody
Chords
G G D7 D7 D7 D7 C G

She wore a yellow ribbon

Plectrum Guitar, Guitarmonk

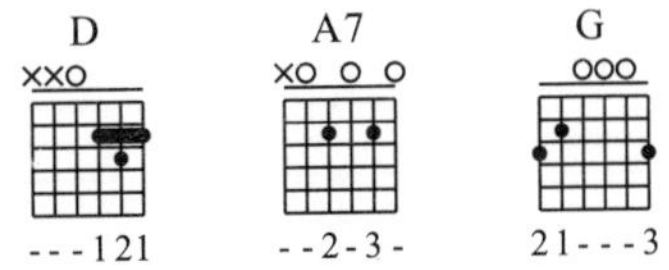

Moderate ♩ = 140

Melody
Chords
D D D D D D D D A7 A7
2
1
Melody
Chords
A7 A7 D D G G G G D D

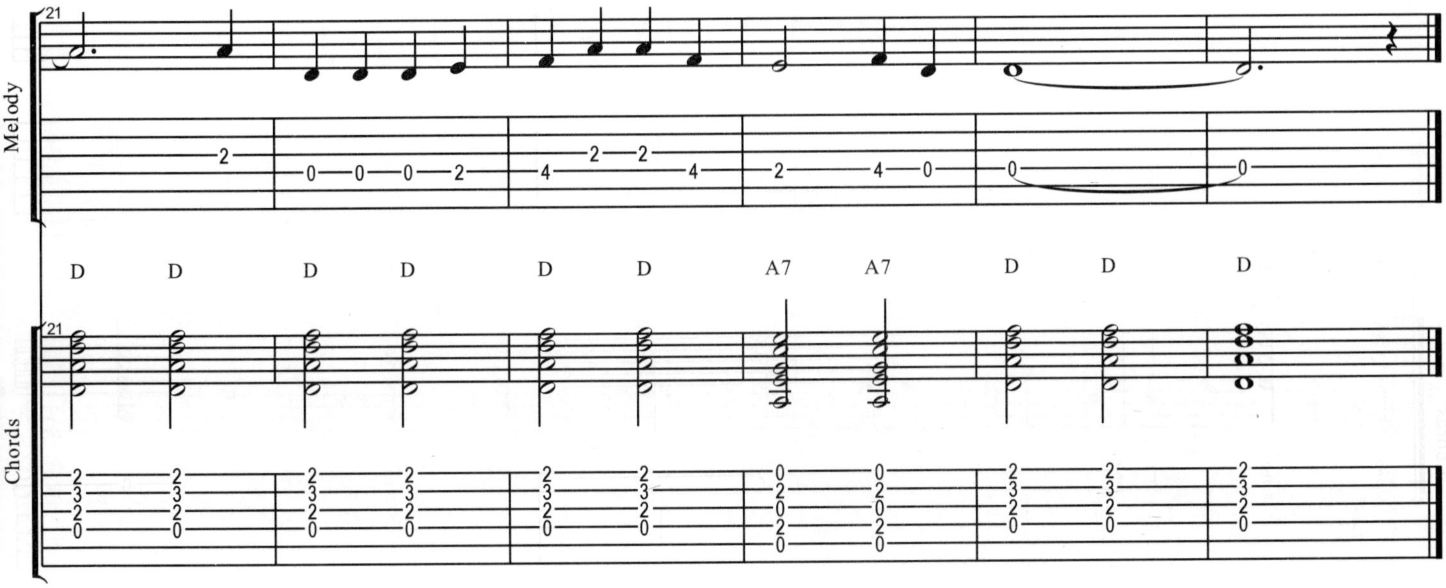
Melody
Chords
D D D D D D A7 A7 D D D

Skip To My Lou

Plectrum Guitar, Guitarmonk

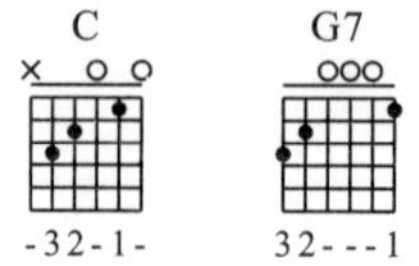

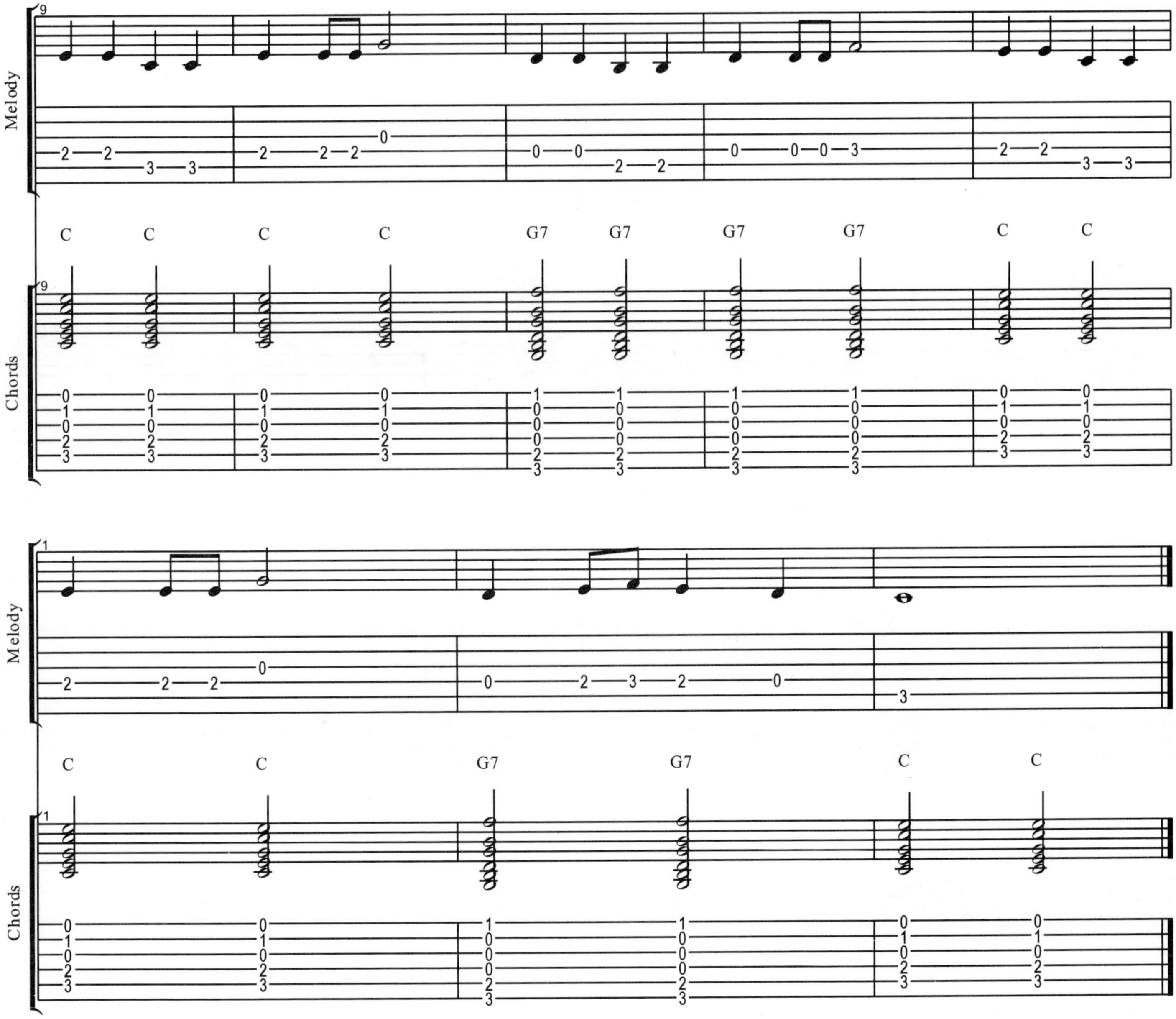
Melody
Chords
C C C C G7 G7 G7 G7 C C
Melody
Chords
C C G7 G7 C C

On Top of Old Smoky

Plectrum Guitar, Guitarmonk

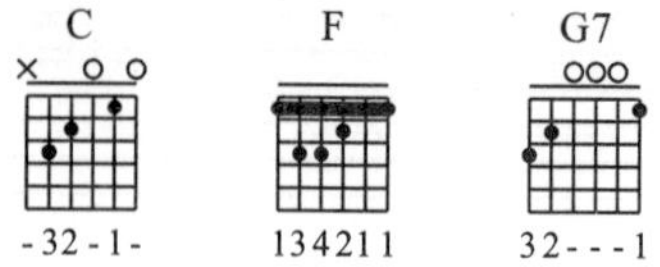

Moderate ♩ = 100

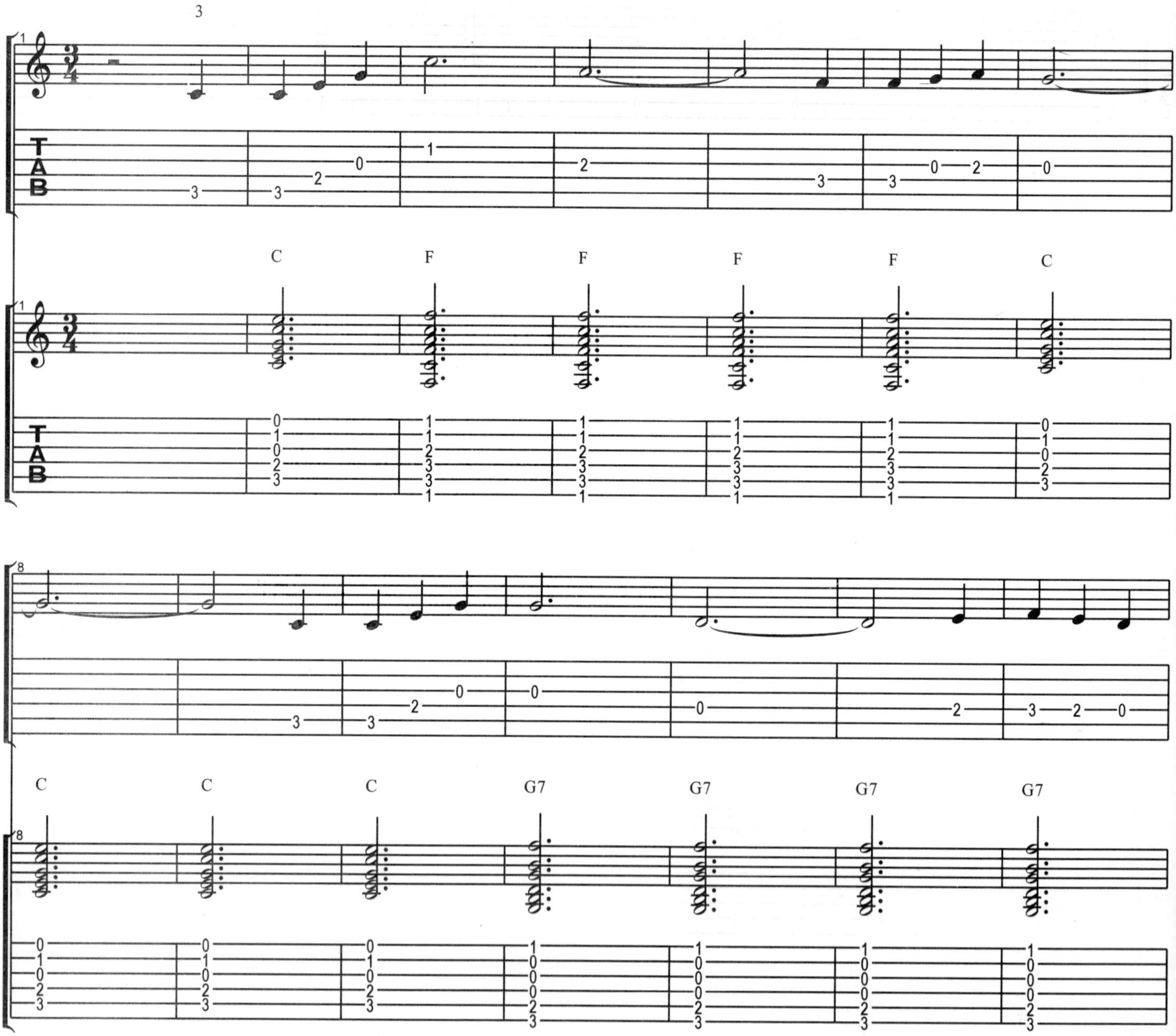

Guitarmonk

INDIAN Pop Songs

MUSIC CHORDS AND LYRICS

(A beautiful repertoire for all music lovers and students ...)

INDIAN SONGS

1. Dooba Dooba
2. Boondein
3. Pal
4. Yaaron
5. Tere Bin Jina Nahin
6. O Sanam
7. Ye Hawa Kehti Hain Kya
8. Purani Jeans

DOOBA DOOBA REHTA HOON

Artist: Mohit Chauhan
Album: Boondein
Scale: F Major

F Bb F
(Dooba Dooba rehta hoon aankhon me teri,
F Bb F
Deewana ban gaya hoon main chaahat me teri), **X 2**
Dm C Dm C
Ab din guzarte nahin, ratein kat-ti nahin,
Dm C Dm C F
Teri tasvir se baat ban-ti nahin..hoooo Aa-ja

Am F
(Koi jaane na, pehchaane na
Dm Bb G C C7
Yeh hua kaise, tum aagaye khwabon mein aise) **X 2**
Dm C Dm C Bb C F
Bewafa, sun oh bewafa, bewafaa, na jaa

F Bb F
(Dooba Dooba rehta hoon aankhon me teri)

Am F Dm Bb
(Tum jo mil gaye, deeye jal gaye, mere khwabon mein
G C C7
Ban jao tum mere humsafar,) X 2
Dm C Dm C Bb C F
Bewafa, sun oh bewafa, bewafaa, na jaa

F Bb F
(Dooba Dooba rehta hoon aankhon me teri,
F Bb F
Deewana ban gaya hoon main chaahat me teri), **X 2**
Dm C Dm C
Ab din guzarte nahin, ratein kat-ti nahin,
Dm C Dm C F
Teri tasvir se baat ban-ti nahin..hoooo Aa-ja
Dm C Dm C Bb C F
Na ja bewafa, bewafa, na jaa, bewafa, aa ja, bewafa, na jaa
F Bb F
La la la la, le aa, la l la, l l

Dooba Dooba Rehta hoon,

Ankhon mein teri,

Deewana ban gaya hoo main,

Chaahat mein teri,

Ab din gujarte nahi,

Ratein kat-ti nahin,

Teri tasveer se,

Baat banti nahi,

Ho...aa jaa..

BOONDEIN

Artist: Mohit Chauhan
Album: Boondein
Scale: F Major

F **F**
Koi ho, yaadon mein,
Am **Bb**
Palko pe boondein liye,
Gm **C**
Aaeina bani,
Bb **C**
Yeh aankhen teri

F **F**
Dheemi si, khusbu hai
Am **Bb**
Haawao ke jhokon ne jo,
Gm **C**
Chuke tujhe,
Bb **C**
Churaaayeee

F **F**
Saanson ki, raahon mein,
Am **C7**
Kya mile sakenge kabhi,
Gm **C**
Dhoonde tujhe,
Bb **C**
Nigahe meri

F **F**
Hoton se, hole se,
Am **Bb**
Sargam jo bahne lagi,
Gm **C**
Aane lagi,
Bb **C**
Chahe meri

F **F**
Saathi the, janmo se,
Am **Bb**
Rahon mein kyu kho gaye,

Gm **C**
Manzil humein,
Bb **C**
Bulane lagi,
F
Hey hey e e he he,

F **F**
Nagma ho, bhiga sa
Am **Bb**
Ya tum ho koi gazal,
Gm **C**
Har pal jise
Bb **C**
Gungunata rahu

F **Bb F**
Hey hey e e he he,
F **Bb C**
Hey, hey a ha ha

Koi ho,

Yaadon mein,

Palko pe boondein liye,

Aaeina bani,

Yeh Aankhen Teri,

Dheemi si,

Khushbu hai,

Haawao ke jhonko ne jo,

Chuke tujhe,

Churaayee...

Saanson ki,

Rahon mein,

Kya milk sakenge kabhi,

Dhoonde tujhe,

Nigahe meri,

PAL

Artist: K.K.
Album: Pal
Scale: E Major

E F#m A B
(Hum rahe ya na rahe kal, kal yaad aayenge yeh pal)

E F#m
Pal, yeh hain pyaar ke pal,
A B
Chal, aa mere sang chal
C#m G#m
Chal, soche kya
F#m B
Chhoti si hai zindagi
C#m G#m F#m B
Kal mil jaaye to hogi khushnaseebi
E F#m B E
Hum rahe ya Na rahe, yaad aayenge yeh pal) – 2

G#m A G#m A
Shaam ka aanchal odhke aayi
F#m B
Dekho voh raat suhaani
G#m A G#m A
Aa likh de hum dono milke
F#m B
Apni yeh prem kahaani

E F#m B E
Hum rahe ya na rahe, yaad aayenge yeh pal)

G#m A G#m A
Aane waali subha jaane
F#m B
Rang kya laaye deewaani
G#m A G#m A
Meri chaahat ko rakh lena
F#m B
Jaise koi nishaani

E F#m B E
Hum rahe ya na rahe, yaad aayenge yeh pal)

Hum Rahe ya na rahe kal,

Kal yaad aayenge yeh pal,

Pal, Yeh hai pyaar ke pal,

chal aa mere sang chal,

Chal, soche kya,

Chhoti si hai zindagi,

Kal mil jaaye to hogi,

Khushnaseebi,

Hum rahe ya Na rahe, yaad,

aayenge yeh pal....

YAARON

4

```
F           Bb  F
Yaaron dosti badi hi haseen hai,
        Dm   Gm       Bb               F
Yeh na ho to kya phir, bolo yeh zindagi hai,
   BbM7        F         F        Bb
Koi to ho raazdaar, be garaj tera ho yaar,
    F          BbM7
Koi to ho raazdaar,

F         Bb        F
Yaaron mohabbat hi to bandagi hai,
       Dm   Gm      Bb              F
Yeh na ho to kya phir bolo yeh zindagi hai,
    BbM7       F      F                Bb
Koi to dilbar ho yaar jisko ho tujhse ho pyaar,
    F             BbM7
Koi to dilbar ho yaar,

Am         Bb         C
Teri har ek buraai pe daante woh dost,
FM7                  Bb
Gam ki ho dhoop,  to saaya bane,
F
tera woh dost,
Bb               F
 Naache bhi woh teri khushi main,


      F   Bb   F
Are Yaaron dosti badi hi haseen hai,
       Dm   Gm      Bb              F
Yeh na ho to kya phir, bolo yeh zindgi hai,
   BbM7        F        F        Bb
Koi to ho raazdaar, be garaj tera ho yaar,
    F          BbM7
Koi to ho raazdaar,

Am              Bb          C
Tan mann kare tum pe fida, mehboob vo,
FM7         Bb          F
Palkon pe jo rakhe tujhe, mehboob vo,
Bb        F
Jiski vafa tere liye ho,
```

Artist: K.K.
Movie: Rockford
Scale: F Major

Arey Yaron...

Dosti badi hi haseen hain,

Yeh na ho to kya phir,

bolo yeh zindagi hain,

Koi to,

Ho razdaar,

Begaraj,

Tera ho yaar,

Koi to, ho razdaar....

```
      F       Bb         F
Arey  Yaaron mohabbat hi to bandagi hai,
       Dm   Gm      Bb              F
Yeh na ho to kya phir bolo yeh zindagi hai,
    BbM7       F      F                Bb
Koi to dilbar ho yaar jisko ho tujhse ho pyaar,
    F             BbM7
Koi to dilbar ho yaar,
```

TERE BIN JEENA NAHIN

Artist: Bali Bhrambhat
Album: Tere Bin Jeena Nahi
Scale: D Major

```
D          Bm           G          A                 D
Tere bin jeena nahi, o meri jaan-e-wafaa

       G                         A                  F#m                D
Zindagi bhar, saath reh kar, mujhe hona nahi hai judaa    X 2
D        Bm            G           A                D
Tere bin jeena nahi, O meri jaan-e-wafaa


D                                     G              C                D
Tu mili toh mujhe mil gayi , zindagi ki har khushi

D     Bm                                    G            C                       D
Jism main hoon meri jaan hai tu, bin tere main kuch nahi
      Bm           G           A                        D
Kahe kya sun zara, aati jaati saanson ki sadaa
D            Bm    G       A                  D
Tere bin jeena nahi, o meri jaan-e-wafaa


 D                                 G              C              D
Zehn mein mere har ghadi, tera hi khayaal hai

D                Bm                        G                C                 D
Tu nahi toh yeh khushiyan sanam , jaise ik malaal hai
          Bm            G            A          D
Aa bhi jaa, aa bhi jaa, sabra ka na le yun imtehan


D            Bm    G       A                   D
Tere bin jeena nahi, o meri jaan-e-wafaa
          G                        A                F#m                  D
Zindagi bhar, saath reh kar, mujhe hona nahi hai judaa
D             Bm  G         A                   D
Tere bin jeena nahi, o meri jaan-e-wafaa
```

Tere Bin,

Jeena Nahi, o meri jaan-e-

Wafaa,

Zindagi bhar,

Saath reh kar,

Mujhe hona nahi hain judaa,

Tere Bin,

Jeena Nahi, o meri jaan-e-

Wafaa....

O SANAM

Artist: Lucky Ali
Album: Sunoh
Scale: G Major

G C A D D7 G
Hmm..mm..   Hmm…mm... Ho..o…

G   Am
Shaam sawere teri yaadein aati hain
G   D
Aake dil ko mere yu tadpati hain
C   Am   D7   G
O Sanam mohabbat ki kasam,

G   Am
Milke bichad na to dastoor ho gaya
G   D
Yadoon mein teri main jo door hogaya
C   Am   D7   G
O Sanam teri yadoon ki kasam

G   Am
Samjhe zamaana ke dil he khilona
Em   D
Jaana hai ab kya hai dil ka lagana
C   D
Nazroon se na yu humko girana
Em   G
Mar bhi gaye toh bhul na jaana.

(O Sanam….)

Shaam Sawere teri,

yaadein Aati hai,

Aake dil ko mere,

Yu tadpati hain,

O sanam,

Mohabat ki kasa,.

Hmm…mmm….

G   Am
Ankhon mein bassee ho, par door ho kaheen
G   D
Dil ke kareeb ho, yeh mujhko hai yakeen
C   Am   D7   G
O Sanam tere pyar ki kasam.

G C A D D7 G
Hmm mm   mm

YE HAWA KEHTI HAI KYA

Artist: Aryans
Album: Ye Hawa Kehti hai Kya
Scale: B Major

B **G#m**
(Yeh hawa, kehti hai kya,
E **F#** **B**
Sun to, meri jaana meri jaana) **X2**
B **G#m**
Yeh fizaa, kehti hai kya,
E **F#** **B**
Sun to, meri jaana, meri jaana, Meri jaana....

B **G#m** **E** **G#m**
(Bin tere mai kaise, jee sakunga, jee sakunga
C#m **F#** **B**
tera pyar kab mai, pa sakunga, pa sakunga) **X2**
B **G#m** **E** **F#** **B**
(Meri dua, chahti hai kya, Tera, pyar jaana, meri jaana)
X2
B
Meri jaana

B **G#m** **E** **G#m**
(Mehki hai fizayein, tu kahan hai,
C#m **F#** **B**
Suni waadiyan hai, tu kahan hai) **X2**
B **G#m** **E** **F#** **B**
(Sun le mere, dil ki sada, aaja, meri jaana, meri jaana) **X2**

Ye Hawa, Kehti Hai kya,

Sun to , meri jaana,

Meri jaana,

Yeh fizaa, kehti hain kya,

Sun to , meri jaana,

Meri jaana,

Bin tere main kaise,

Jee sakunga,

Tera pyaar kab main,

Paa sakunga..

B **G#m**
Yeh hawa, kehti hai kya,
E **F#** **B**
Sun to, meri jaana meri jaana
B
Meri jaana., Meri jaana, Meri jaana, Meri jaana.

PURANI JEANS

8

Artist: Ali Header
Album: Sandesha
Scale: C# Major

C#
Purani jeans aur guitar,
F# C#
Mohalle ki vo chat, aur mere yaar, vo raaton ko jaagna,
F# C#
Subah ghar jaana , kood ke deewar,
A#m F#
Vo cigaretee peena , gali mein jaake,
G# C#
Wo karna daanton ko, ghadi ghadi saaf,
C#
Pahunchna college hamesha late,
F# C#
Vo kehna sir ka , "get out from the class!"

Vo bahar jaake hamsha kehna,
F# C#
Yahan ka system, hi hai kharaab,
A#m F#
Vo jaake canteen mein, Table bajaake,
G# C#
Vo gaane gaana, Yaaron ke saath,
C#
Bas yaadein, Yaadein, Yaadein reh jaati hain,
G# C#
Kuchh chhoti, chhoti, baatein reh jaati hain, bas yaadein..

Purani Jeans

Aur Guitar

Mohalle ki vo chat,

Aur mere Yaar,

Aisa yaadon ka mausam chala,

Bhoolta hi nahin, dil mera,

(Purani Jeans...)

C# F#
Vo papa ka daantna, vo kehna mummy ka,
C#
Chhodein ji aap, tumhein to bas nazar aata hain,
F# C#
Jahan mein beta, mera hi kharaab,
A#m F#
Vo dil mein sochna, kar ke kuchh dikha dein,
G# C#
Vo karna planning, roz nayi yaar,

C# F#
Vo khidki se jhaankna, vo likhna letter,
C# A#m
Unhein baar baar, vo dena tofe mein,
F# G#
Sone ki baaliyan, vo lena doston se,
C#
Paise udhaar...,

C# A#m
Ladakpan ka vo pehla pyaar,
F# C#
Vo likhna haathon pe A + R,

C#
Bas yaadein, Yaadein, Yaadein reh jaati hain,
G# C#
Kuchh chhoti, chhoti, baatein reh jaati hain, bas yaadein..